50 Tuna Recipes for Home

By: Kelly Johnson

Table of Contents

- Tuna Nicoise Salad
- Tuna Melt Sandwich
- Grilled Tuna Steaks with Lemon and Garlic
- Tuna Pasta Salad
- Spicy Tuna Sushi Rolls
- Tuna and Avocado Wrap
- Mediterranean Tuna Casserole
- Tuna Ceviche
- Tuna Stuffed Bell Peppers
- Tuna and White Bean Salad
- Tuna and Capers Pizza
- Tuna Patties with Dill Sauce
- Tuna and Corn Quesadillas
- Tuna and Broccoli Stir-Fry
- Tuna and Chickpea Salad
- Tuna and Spinach Stuffed Mushrooms
- Tuna and Zucchini Fritters
- Tuna and Olive Tapenade Crostini
- Tuna and Quinoa Bowl
- Tuna and Sundried Tomato Pesto Pasta
- Tuna and Potato Hash
- Tuna and Cucumber Rolls
- Tuna and Artichoke Dip
- Tuna and Egg Breakfast Burrito
- Tuna and Rice Stuffed Tomatoes
- Tuna and Fennel Salad
- Tuna and Corn Chowder
- Tuna and Mango Salsa Tacos
- Tuna and Pesto Stuffed Peppers
- Tuna and Lemon Risotto
- Tuna and Watermelon Salad
- Tuna and Asparagus Quiche
- Tuna and Mushroom Stroganoff
- Tuna and Roasted Red Pepper Sandwich
- Tuna and Green Bean Almondine

- Tuna and Dill Cucumber Bites
- Tuna and Pineapple Skewers
- Tuna and Sweet Potato Hash
- Tuna and Roasted Garlic Hummus Wrap
- Tuna and Cilantro Lime Rice Bowl
- Tuna and Blue Cheese Flatbread
- Tuna and Mango Avocado Rolls
- Tuna and Cornbread Casserole
- Tuna and Cranberry Quinoa Salad
- Tuna and Tomato Bruschetta
- Tuna and Basil Pesto Panini
- Tuna and Roasted Vegetable Salad
- Tuna and Bacon Stuffed Mushrooms
- Tuna and Black Bean Burrito Bowl
- Tuna and Orange Glazed Salmon Skewers

Tuna Nicoise Salad

Ingredients:

- 1 pound small red potatoes, halved
- 8 ounces green beans, trimmed
- 4 large eggs
- 1/4 cup Niçoise olives, pitted
- 1 cup cherry tomatoes, halved
- 4 cups mixed salad greens
- 1/4 cup capers, drained
- 1/4 cup fresh parsley, chopped
- 2 tablespoons red onion, thinly sliced
- 2 tablespoons Dijon mustard
- 2 tablespoons red wine vinegar
- 1/3 cup extra-virgin olive oil
- Salt and pepper to taste
- 2 (5-ounce) cans of tuna, drained

Instructions:

Boil Potatoes: Place the halved potatoes in a pot of salted water. Bring to a boil and cook until fork-tender, about 10-15 minutes. Drain and set aside.

Blanch Green Beans: In the same pot, add the green beans and cook for 2-3 minutes until they are bright green and crisp-tender. Immediately transfer them to a bowl of ice water to stop the cooking process.

Hard-Boil Eggs: Place the eggs in a saucepan and cover with water. Bring to a boil, then reduce the heat and simmer for 8-10 minutes. Transfer the eggs to ice water and peel them. Cut each egg in half.

Assemble Salad: Arrange the salad greens on a platter. Arrange the cooked potatoes, green beans, hard-boiled eggs, olives, cherry tomatoes, capers, and tuna on top.

Prepare Dressing: In a small bowl, whisk together Dijon mustard, red wine vinegar, olive oil, salt, and pepper. Drizzle the dressing over the salad.

Garnish: Sprinkle chopped parsley and thinly sliced red onion over the salad for added flavor.

Serve: Serve the Tuna Nicoise Salad immediately, allowing each person to mix their own salad or serve pre-mixed portions onto individual plates.

This Tuna Nicoise Salad is not only visually appealing but also a delicious and satisfying meal that brings together the flavors of tuna, vegetables, and a tangy vinaigrette. Enjoy!

Tuna Melt Sandwich

Ingredients:

- 2 cans (about 10 oz each) tuna, drained
- 1/3 cup mayonnaise
- 2 tablespoons Dijon mustard
- 1/4 cup red onion, finely chopped
- 1/4 cup celery, finely chopped
- Salt and pepper, to taste
- 4 slices of your favorite bread
- 4 slices Swiss or cheddar cheese
- Butter, for spreading

Instructions:

In a mixing bowl, combine the drained tuna, mayonnaise, Dijon mustard, red onion, and celery. Stir until well combined.
Season the tuna mixture with salt and pepper according to your taste. Set aside.
Preheat a skillet or griddle over medium heat.
Butter one side of each slice of bread.
Place two slices of bread, butter side down, on the skillet.
Divide the tuna mixture evenly onto the two slices of bread in the skillet.
Top each tuna-covered slice with a slice of cheese.
Place the remaining slices of bread on top, butter side up.
Cook until the bread is golden brown and the cheese is melted, about 3-4 minutes per side.
Carefully flip the sandwiches using a spatula to ensure even cooking on both sides.
Once both sides are golden brown and the cheese is melted, remove the sandwiches from the skillet.
Allow them to cool for a minute before slicing in half.
Serve the tuna melt sandwiches warm with your favorite sides or a simple green salad.

Enjoy your delicious Tuna Melt Sandwich!

Grilled Tuna Steaks with Lemon and Garlic

Ingredients:

- 4 tuna steaks (about 6 oz each)
- 1/4 cup olive oil
- 3 cloves garlic, minced
- Zest of 1 lemon
- Juice of 1 lemon
- 1 teaspoon dried oregano
- 1 teaspoon dried thyme
- Salt and pepper, to taste
- Lemon wedges, for serving
- Fresh parsley, chopped, for garnish

Instructions:

Preheat your grill to medium-high heat.

In a small bowl, whisk together the olive oil, minced garlic, lemon zest, lemon juice, dried oregano, dried thyme, salt, and pepper to create the marinade.

Pat the tuna steaks dry with paper towels and place them in a shallow dish.

Pour half of the marinade over the tuna steaks, making sure each steak is well-coated. Let them marinate for at least 15-20 minutes, allowing the flavors to infuse.

While the tuna is marinating, brush the grill grates with a bit of oil to prevent sticking.

Place the marinated tuna steaks on the preheated grill. Cook for about 2-3 minutes per side for medium-rare, or adjust the cooking time according to your preference.

Baste the tuna steaks with the remaining marinade during grilling to enhance the flavors.

Once the tuna steaks are grilled to your liking, remove them from the grill and transfer to a serving platter.

Garnish with chopped fresh parsley and serve immediately with lemon wedges on the side.

Enjoy the Grilled Tuna Steaks with Lemon and Garlic alongside your favorite grilled vegetables or a light salad.

This recipe provides a delightful combination of citrusy and herby flavors that complement the richness of the tuna.

Tuna Pasta Salad

Ingredients:

For the Salad:

- 8 oz (about 2 cups) rotini or your favorite pasta, cooked and cooled
- 2 cans (about 10 oz each) tuna, drained
- 1 cup cherry tomatoes, halved
- 1/2 cucumber, diced
- 1/2 red bell pepper, diced
- 1/4 cup red onion, finely chopped
- 1/4 cup black olives, sliced
- 1/4 cup feta cheese, crumbled (optional)

For the Dressing:

- 1/3 cup olive oil
- 3 tablespoons red wine vinegar
- 1 clove garlic, minced
- 1 teaspoon Dijon mustard
- 1 teaspoon honey
- Salt and pepper, to taste

Instructions:

In a large mixing bowl, combine the cooked and cooled pasta, drained tuna, cherry tomatoes, cucumber, red bell pepper, red onion, black olives, and feta cheese (if using).
In a separate bowl, whisk together the olive oil, red wine vinegar, minced garlic, Dijon mustard, honey, salt, and pepper to create the dressing.
Pour the dressing over the pasta and tuna mixture. Gently toss until everything is well coated.
Cover the bowl with plastic wrap and refrigerate for at least 30 minutes to allow the flavors to meld.
Before serving, give the pasta salad a final toss and adjust the seasoning if necessary.

Serve the Tuna Pasta Salad chilled, garnished with additional feta cheese and fresh herbs if desired.

This refreshing and flavorful Tuna Pasta Salad is perfect for picnics, potlucks, or a light lunch. Enjoy!

Spicy Tuna Sushi Rolls

Ingredients:

For the Spicy Tuna Filling:

- 2 cans (about 10 oz each) tuna in water, drained
- 2 tablespoons mayonnaise
- 1 tablespoon Sriracha sauce (adjust to taste)
- 1 teaspoon sesame oil
- 1 teaspoon soy sauce
- 1 green onion, finely chopped
- 1/2 teaspoon sesame seeds
- Salt and pepper, to taste

For the Sushi Rolls:

- 2 cups sushi rice, cooked and seasoned with rice vinegar, sugar, and salt
- 10 sheets of nori (seaweed)
- 1 cucumber, julienned
- 1 avocado, sliced
- Soy sauce, for dipping
- Pickled ginger and wasabi, for serving

Instructions:

For the Spicy Tuna Filling:

In a bowl, combine drained tuna, mayonnaise, Sriracha sauce, sesame oil, soy sauce, green onion, sesame seeds, salt, and pepper. Mix well until all ingredients are evenly incorporated. Adjust Sriracha according to your desired spice level.

For the Sushi Rolls:

Place a bamboo sushi rolling mat on a flat surface. Lay a sheet of nori, shiny side down, on the mat.

Wet your fingers to prevent sticking and spread a thin layer of sushi rice evenly over the nori, leaving about half an inch at the top edge.

Place a line of the spicy tuna filling horizontally across the center of the rice.

Add julienned cucumber and sliced avocado alongside the tuna filling.

Starting from the bottom, lift the bamboo mat and roll the nori tightly over the filling. Seal the edge with a little water.

Repeat the process with the remaining ingredients.

Once you've rolled all the sushi, use a sharp knife to slice each roll into bite-sized pieces.

Serve the Spicy Tuna Sushi Rolls with soy sauce, pickled ginger, and wasabi.

Enjoy these delicious and flavorful spicy tuna sushi rolls as a snack or part of a sushi night at home!

Tuna and Avocado Wrap

Ingredients:

For the Tuna Filling:

- 2 cans (about 10 oz each) tuna, drained
- 2 tablespoons mayonnaise
- 1 tablespoon Dijon mustard
- 1 tablespoon lemon juice
- 1/4 cup red onion, finely chopped
- Salt and pepper, to taste

For the Wrap:

- 4 large whole wheat or spinach tortillas
- 2 ripe avocados, sliced
- 1 cup cherry tomatoes, halved
- 1 cup lettuce or spinach leaves, washed and dried
- 1/2 cup shredded carrots
- 1/4 cup fresh cilantro, chopped (optional)

Instructions:

For the Tuna Filling:

In a bowl, combine drained tuna, mayonnaise, Dijon mustard, lemon juice, red onion, salt, and pepper. Mix well until all ingredients are evenly incorporated.

Assembling the Wrap:

Lay out the tortillas on a flat surface.
Divide the tuna filling evenly among the tortillas, spreading it in the center.
Add slices of avocado, halved cherry tomatoes, lettuce or spinach leaves, shredded carrots, and chopped cilantro (if using) over the tuna filling.
Fold in the sides of each tortilla and then roll it up tightly, creating a wrap.
Slice each wrap in half diagonally for easier handling.

Serve the Tuna and Avocado Wraps immediately, or wrap them in parchment paper or foil for an on-the-go lunch.

Enjoy these delicious and nutritious tuna and avocado wraps as a satisfying meal or a portable lunch option!

Mediterranean Tuna Casserole

Ingredients:

For the Casserole:

- 8 oz penne or your favorite pasta, cooked according to package instructions
- 2 cans (about 10 oz each) tuna, drained
- 1 cup cherry tomatoes, halved
- 1/2 cup Kalamata olives, pitted and sliced
- 1/2 cup artichoke hearts, chopped
- 1/2 cup red bell pepper, diced
- 1/4 cup red onion, finely chopped
- 1/4 cup fresh parsley, chopped
- 1 cup feta cheese, crumbled

For the Sauce:

- 3 tablespoons olive oil
- 3 cloves garlic, minced
- 1 teaspoon dried oregano
- 1 teaspoon dried basil
- 1/2 teaspoon dried thyme
- Salt and pepper, to taste
- 1 can (14 oz) diced tomatoes, drained

Instructions:

Preheat your oven to 375°F (190°C).

For the Sauce:

In a medium saucepan, heat olive oil over medium heat. Add minced garlic and sauté until fragrant.
Stir in dried oregano, dried basil, dried thyme, salt, and pepper. Cook for an additional minute.

Add drained diced tomatoes to the saucepan, stirring to combine. Simmer for 5-7 minutes until the sauce thickens slightly. Set aside.

Assembling the Casserole:

In a large mixing bowl, combine cooked pasta, drained tuna, cherry tomatoes, Kalamata olives, artichoke hearts, red bell pepper, red onion, and fresh parsley. Pour the prepared sauce over the pasta mixture and toss until everything is well coated.
Transfer the mixture to a baking dish and spread it evenly.
Sprinkle crumbled feta cheese over the top of the casserole.
Bake in the preheated oven for 20-25 minutes or until the cheese is melted, and the casserole is heated through.
Remove from the oven and let it rest for a few minutes before serving.
Garnish with additional fresh parsley if desired and serve this Mediterranean Tuna Casserole warm.
Enjoy the flavorful blend of Mediterranean ingredients in this delicious and hearty casserole!

Tuna Ceviche

Ingredients:

- 1 lb fresh sushi-grade tuna, diced into bite-sized cubes
- 1/2 cup red onion, finely chopped
- 1 jalapeño, seeds removed and finely diced
- 1 cup cherry tomatoes, quartered
- 1/2 cup cucumber, diced
- 1/4 cup cilantro, chopped
- 1/4 cup green onions, finely sliced
- Juice of 4-5 limes
- Juice of 2 lemons
- 2 tablespoons orange juice
- 2 tablespoons soy sauce
- 1 tablespoon honey or agave syrup
- Salt and pepper, to taste
- Avocado slices, for garnish
- Tortilla chips or plantain chips, for serving

Instructions:

In a large glass or stainless steel bowl, combine the diced tuna, red onion, jalapeño, cherry tomatoes, cucumber, cilantro, and green onions.
In a separate bowl, whisk together the lime juice, lemon juice, orange juice, soy sauce, honey, salt, and pepper to create the ceviche marinade.
Pour the marinade over the tuna mixture, ensuring all ingredients are well coated. Toss gently to combine.
Cover the bowl with plastic wrap and refrigerate for at least 30 minutes to allow the flavors to meld and the tuna to "cook" in the citrus juices.
Before serving, taste and adjust the seasoning if needed.
Serve the tuna ceviche in individual bowls, garnished with avocado slices.
Accompany with tortilla chips or plantain chips for scooping up the delicious ceviche.
Enjoy this refreshing and vibrant Tuna Ceviche as a light appetizer or a flavorful snack!

Tuna Stuffed Bell Peppers

Ingredients:

For the Stuffed Bell Peppers:

- 4 large bell peppers, halved and seeds removed
- 2 cans (about 10 oz each) tuna, drained
- 1 cup cooked quinoa or rice
- 1 cup cherry tomatoes, diced
- 1/2 cup black olives, sliced
- 1/4 cup red onion, finely chopped
- 1/4 cup feta cheese, crumbled
- 2 cloves garlic, minced
- 2 tablespoons fresh parsley, chopped
- Salt and pepper, to taste

For the Tomato Sauce:

- 1 can (14 oz) diced tomatoes
- 2 tablespoons tomato paste
- 1 teaspoon dried oregano
- 1 teaspoon dried basil
- 1/2 teaspoon garlic powder
- Salt and pepper, to taste

Instructions:

For the Stuffed Bell Peppers:

Preheat the oven to 375°F (190°C).
In a large mixing bowl, combine the drained tuna, cooked quinoa or rice, diced cherry tomatoes, sliced black olives, red onion, feta cheese, minced garlic, chopped parsley, salt, and pepper. Mix well.
Place the bell pepper halves in a baking dish.
Spoon the tuna mixture evenly into each bell pepper half, pressing it down gently.

For the Tomato Sauce:

In a blender or food processor, combine the diced tomatoes, tomato paste, dried oregano, dried basil, garlic powder, salt, and pepper. Blend until smooth.

Pour the tomato sauce over the stuffed bell peppers in the baking dish.

Cover the dish with aluminum foil and bake for 25-30 minutes, or until the bell peppers are tender.

Remove the foil and bake for an additional 5-10 minutes until the tops are slightly golden.

Remove from the oven and let the stuffed bell peppers cool for a few minutes before serving.

Garnish with additional fresh parsley if desired.

Serve the Tuna Stuffed Bell Peppers warm, and enjoy a nutritious and flavorful meal!

These stuffed bell peppers make for a delicious and wholesome dish, combining the goodness of tuna, quinoa or rice, and a tasty tomato sauce.

Tuna and White Bean Salad

Ingredients:

For the Salad:

- 2 cans (about 10 oz each) tuna, drained
- 2 cans (15 oz each) white beans (cannellini or great northern), drained and rinsed
- 1 cup cherry tomatoes, halved
- 1/2 cup red onion, finely chopped
- 1/4 cup Kalamata olives, pitted and sliced
- 1/4 cup fresh parsley, chopped
- 1/4 cup fresh basil, chopped
- 1/4 cup feta cheese, crumbled (optional)
- Salt and pepper, to taste

For the Dressing:

- 1/4 cup extra-virgin olive oil
- 2 tablespoons red wine vinegar
- 1 teaspoon Dijon mustard
- 1 clove garlic, minced
- 1 teaspoon honey
- Salt and pepper, to taste

Instructions:

For the Salad:

In a large mixing bowl, combine the drained tuna, white beans, cherry tomatoes, red onion, Kalamata olives, fresh parsley, fresh basil, and feta cheese (if using). Season with salt and pepper according to your taste. Toss gently to combine.

For the Dressing:

In a small bowl, whisk together the extra-virgin olive oil, red wine vinegar, Dijon mustard, minced garlic, honey, salt, and pepper.
Pour the dressing over the tuna and white bean mixture. Toss until everything is well coated.

Allow the salad to marinate in the refrigerator for at least 30 minutes to let the flavors meld.

Before serving, give the salad a final toss and adjust the seasoning if necessary.

Serve the Tuna and White Bean Salad chilled, either on its own or over a bed of mixed greens.

Enjoy this protein-packed and flavorful salad as a light lunch or dinner option!

Tuna and Capers Pizza

Ingredients:

For the Pizza Dough:

- 1 pound pizza dough (store-bought or homemade)

For the Topping:

- 1 can (about 10 oz) tuna in water, drained
- 2 tablespoons olive oil
- 2 cloves garlic, minced
- 1/2 cup tomato sauce
- 1 teaspoon dried oregano
- Salt and pepper, to taste
- 1 cup mozzarella cheese, shredded
- 1/4 cup red onion, thinly sliced
- 2 tablespoons capers, drained
- Fresh basil leaves, for garnish

Instructions:

Preheat your oven to the temperature recommended for your pizza dough.

For the Pizza Dough:

If using store-bought dough, follow the package instructions for rolling and baking. If making homemade dough, roll it out on a floured surface to your desired thickness.

For the Topping:

In a small pan, heat olive oil over medium heat. Add minced garlic and sauté for about 1 minute until fragrant. Be careful not to brown the garlic.
Add the drained tuna to the pan and cook for an additional 2-3 minutes, breaking it up with a fork. Season with salt and pepper. Remove from heat.

Spread tomato sauce evenly over the rolled-out pizza dough.
Sprinkle dried oregano over the sauce.
Evenly distribute the sautéed tuna and garlic mixture over the sauce.
Sprinkle shredded mozzarella cheese over the top.
Scatter thinly sliced red onions and capers across the pizza.
Place the pizza on a preheated pizza stone or directly on a baking sheet.
Bake in the preheated oven according to the dough instructions or until the crust is golden and the cheese is melted and bubbly.
Remove from the oven, garnish with fresh basil leaves, and let it cool for a few minutes before slicing.
Serve the Tuna and Capers Pizza hot, and enjoy this unique and flavorful twist on traditional pizza!

Tuna Patties with Dill Sauce

For the Tuna Patties:

Ingredients:

- 2 cans (about 10 oz each) tuna, drained
- 2 cups mashed potatoes (leftover or freshly made and cooled)
- 1/2 cup breadcrumbs
- 1/4 cup red onion, finely chopped
- 2 cloves garlic, minced
- 1/4 cup fresh parsley, chopped
- 1 teaspoon Dijon mustard
- 2 eggs, beaten
- Salt and pepper, to taste
- Olive oil, for frying

For the Dill Sauce:

Ingredients:

- 1/2 cup mayonnaise
- 2 tablespoons Greek yogurt or sour cream
- 1 tablespoon fresh dill, chopped
- 1 tablespoon lemon juice
- Salt and pepper, to taste

Instructions:

For the Tuna Patties:

> In a large mixing bowl, combine the drained tuna, mashed potatoes, breadcrumbs, red onion, minced garlic, chopped fresh parsley, Dijon mustard, beaten eggs, salt, and pepper. Mix well until all ingredients are evenly incorporated.
> Shape the mixture into patties, about 3-4 inches in diameter, and place them on a tray or plate.
> Heat olive oil in a skillet over medium heat.
> Carefully place the tuna patties in the hot skillet and cook for 3-4 minutes on each side, or until golden brown and cooked through.

Once cooked, transfer the tuna patties to a plate lined with paper towels to absorb any excess oil.

For the Dill Sauce:

In a small bowl, whisk together mayonnaise, Greek yogurt or sour cream, chopped fresh dill, lemon juice, salt, and pepper. Adjust the seasoning to taste. Serve the Tuna Patties with the Dill Sauce on the side for dipping or drizzling. Garnish with additional fresh dill or parsley if desired.
Enjoy these Tuna Patties with Dill Sauce as a delightful and satisfying meal!

Tuna and Corn Quesadillas

Ingredients:

- 1 can of tuna, drained
- 1 cup frozen corn, thawed
- 1 cup shredded cheese (cheddar, Monterey Jack, or a blend)
- 1/2 cup diced red onion
- 1/4 cup chopped fresh cilantro
- 1 teaspoon ground cumin
- 1/2 teaspoon chili powder
- Salt and pepper to taste
- 4 large flour tortillas
- Cooking spray or olive oil for cooking
- Optional toppings: salsa, sour cream, guacamole

Instructions:

In a mixing bowl, combine the drained tuna, thawed corn, shredded cheese, diced red onion, chopped cilantro, ground cumin, chili powder, salt, and pepper. Mix everything well to ensure even distribution of flavors.
Place one flour tortilla on a clean surface, and spread a quarter of the tuna and corn mixture evenly over half of the tortilla, leaving some space around the edges.
Fold the other half of the tortilla over the filling, creating a half-moon shape.
Heat a skillet or griddle over medium heat. Lightly coat the surface with cooking spray or a small amount of olive oil.

Carefully transfer the filled tortilla to the heated skillet and cook for 2-3 minutes on each side, or until the tortilla becomes golden brown and the cheese is melted.

Repeat the process for the remaining tortillas and filling.

Once cooked, remove the quesadillas from the skillet and let them cool for a minute before slicing them into wedges.

Serve the tuna and corn quesadillas with your favorite toppings, such as salsa, sour cream, or guacamole.

These quesadillas are versatile, and you can customize them according to your taste preferences. Feel free to add other ingredients like diced tomatoes, jalapeños, or black beans for additional flavor and texture. Enjoy your delicious tuna and corn quesadillas!

Tuna and Broccoli Stir-Fry

Ingredients:

- 2 cans of tuna, drained
- 3 cups broccoli florets
- 1 red bell pepper, sliced
- 1 carrot, julienned
- 3 cloves garlic, minced
- 1 tablespoon ginger, grated
- 3 tablespoons soy sauce
- 1 tablespoon oyster sauce
- 1 tablespoon sesame oil
- 1 tablespoon vegetable oil
- 1 tablespoon cornstarch (optional, for thickening)
- Cooked rice or noodles for serving

Instructions:

In a small bowl, mix together the soy sauce, oyster sauce, and sesame oil. Set aside.
Heat vegetable oil in a large wok or skillet over medium-high heat.
Add minced garlic and grated ginger to the hot oil. Stir-fry for about 30 seconds until fragrant.
Add broccoli florets, sliced red bell pepper, and julienned carrot to the wok. Stir-fry the vegetables for 3-5 minutes until they are slightly tender but still crisp.
Add drained tuna to the wok and continue to stir-fry for an additional 2-3 minutes, allowing the tuna to heat through and absorb the flavors.
Pour the prepared sauce over the tuna and vegetables. Toss everything together to ensure an even coating.
If you prefer a thicker sauce, mix cornstarch with a little water to create a slurry. Stir the slurry into the wok and cook until the sauce thickens.
Once everything is well combined and heated through, remove the wok from the heat.
Serve the tuna and broccoli stir-fry over cooked rice or noodles.

Feel free to customize this recipe by adding other vegetables like snap peas, mushrooms, or baby corn. You can also adjust the seasoning to suit your taste. Enjoy your quick and delicious tuna and broccoli stir-fry!

Tuna and Chickpea Salad

Ingredients:

- 1 can (about 15 ounces) chickpeas, drained and rinsed
- 2 cans (about 5 ounces each) tuna, drained
- 1 cup cherry tomatoes, halved
- 1 cucumber, diced
- 1/2 red onion, finely chopped
- 1/4 cup Kalamata olives, sliced (optional)
- 1/4 cup feta cheese, crumbled (optional)
- 1/4 cup fresh parsley, chopped
- 3 tablespoons extra-virgin olive oil
- 2 tablespoons red wine vinegar
- 1 teaspoon Dijon mustard
- Salt and pepper to taste
- Lemon wedges for serving (optional)

Instructions:

In a large mixing bowl, combine the chickpeas, drained tuna, cherry tomatoes, cucumber, red onion, olives (if using), feta cheese (if using), and fresh parsley.
In a small bowl or jar, whisk together the olive oil, red wine vinegar, Dijon mustard, salt, and pepper to create the dressing.
Pour the dressing over the salad and toss gently to ensure everything is well coated.
Taste the salad and adjust the seasoning if needed.
Allow the tuna and chickpea salad to marinate in the refrigerator for at least 15-20 minutes to let the flavors meld.
Before serving, give the salad a final toss and garnish with additional parsley if desired.
Serve the tuna and chickpea salad on a bed of mixed greens, as a sandwich filling, or simply on its own.
Optionally, serve with lemon wedges on the side for an extra burst of citrus flavor.

This versatile salad is not only delicious but also a great source of protein and fiber. Feel free to customize it by adding other vegetables or herbs based on your preferences. Enjoy your tasty and nutritious tuna and chickpea salad!

Tuna and Spinach Stuffed Mushrooms

Ingredients:

- 12-16 large mushrooms, cleaned and stems removed
- 1 can (about 5 ounces) tuna, drained
- 1 cup fresh spinach, chopped
- 1/4 cup mayonnaise
- 1/4 cup grated Parmesan cheese
- 2 cloves garlic, minced
- 1 teaspoon lemon juice
- Salt and pepper to taste
- 2 tablespoons breadcrumbs (optional, for topping)
- Fresh parsley, chopped (for garnish)

Instructions:

Preheat your oven to 375°F (190°C).
Clean the mushrooms and remove the stems. Place the mushroom caps on a baking sheet lined with parchment paper.
In a mixing bowl, combine drained tuna, chopped fresh spinach, mayonnaise, grated Parmesan cheese, minced garlic, lemon juice, salt, and pepper. Mix everything until well combined.
Spoon the tuna and spinach mixture into each mushroom cap, pressing it down slightly.
If desired, sprinkle breadcrumbs over the top of each stuffed mushroom for a crispy texture.
Bake the stuffed mushrooms in the preheated oven for about 15-20 minutes or until the mushrooms are tender and the filling is heated through.
Once cooked, remove from the oven and garnish with freshly chopped parsley. Allow the stuffed mushrooms to cool for a few minutes before serving.

These tuna and spinach stuffed mushrooms are a flavorful and low-carb option for appetizers or a light meal. They can be served warm or at room temperature. Enjoy this delicious and nutritious dish!

Tuna and Zucchini Fritters

Ingredients:

- 2 medium-sized zucchinis, grated
- 1 can (about 5 ounces) tuna, drained
- 1/2 cup breadcrumbs
- 1/4 cup grated Parmesan cheese
- 2 green onions, finely chopped
- 2 cloves garlic, minced
- 2 large eggs, beaten
- 1 teaspoon dried oregano
- Salt and pepper to taste
- Olive oil for frying

Instructions:

Place the grated zucchini in a clean kitchen towel or cheesecloth and squeeze out excess moisture.
In a large mixing bowl, combine the squeezed zucchini, drained tuna, breadcrumbs, Parmesan cheese, chopped green onions, minced garlic, beaten eggs, dried oregano, salt, and pepper. Mix everything well until evenly combined.
Heat a thin layer of olive oil in a large skillet over medium heat.
Scoop a portion of the mixture and shape it into a patty. Place it in the skillet and flatten it slightly with a spatula. Repeat with the remaining mixture, making sure not to overcrowd the pan.
Cook the fritters for 3-4 minutes on each side or until they are golden brown and cooked through.
Once cooked, transfer the fritters to a paper towel-lined plate to absorb any excess oil.
Serve the tuna and zucchini fritters warm with your favorite dipping sauce or a dollop of Greek yogurt.

These fritters make a delicious and protein-packed snack or light meal. Feel free to customize the recipe by adding herbs, spices, or additional ingredients according to your taste preferences. Enjoy your tuna and zucchini fritters!

Tuna and Olive Tapenade Crostini

Ingredients:

For the Tuna Mixture:

- 1 can (about 5 ounces) tuna, drained
- 2 tablespoons mayonnaise
- 1 tablespoon Dijon mustard
- 1 tablespoon lemon juice
- Salt and pepper to taste

For the Olive Tapenade:

- 1 cup pitted Kalamata olives
- 2 tablespoons capers
- 2 cloves garlic, minced
- 2 tablespoons fresh parsley, chopped
- 1 tablespoon lemon juice
- 3 tablespoons extra-virgin olive oil

For the Crostini:

- Baguette, sliced into 1/2-inch thick rounds
- Olive oil for brushing
- Salt and pepper to taste

Instructions:

Tuna Mixture:
- In a bowl, combine the drained tuna, mayonnaise, Dijon mustard, lemon juice, salt, and pepper. Mix until well combined. Set aside.

Olive Tapenade:
- In a food processor, combine the Kalamata olives, capers, minced garlic, chopped parsley, and lemon juice. Pulse until the mixture is finely chopped.

- While the food processor is running, slowly drizzle in the olive oil until the tapenade reaches your desired consistency.

Crostini:
- Preheat the oven to 375°F (190°C).
- Place the baguette slices on a baking sheet. Brush each slice with olive oil and sprinkle with a pinch of salt and pepper.
- Bake in the preheated oven for about 8-10 minutes or until the crostini is golden and crispy.

Assembling:
- Spread a generous amount of the tuna mixture onto each crostini.
- Top the tuna mixture with a dollop of olive tapenade.
- Optionally, garnish with additional chopped parsley for a fresh touch.

Serve:
- Arrange the tuna and olive tapenade crostini on a serving platter and serve immediately.

This appetizer is not only delicious but also visually appealing, making it perfect for entertaining. Adjust the quantities and ingredients to suit your preferences, and enjoy the flavors of the Mediterranean in each bite!

Tuna and Quinoa Bowl

Ingredients:

For the Tuna:

- 1 can (about 5 ounces) tuna, drained
- 1 tablespoon olive oil
- 1 teaspoon lemon juice
- Salt and pepper to taste

For the Quinoa:

- 1 cup quinoa
- 2 cups water or vegetable broth
- 1/2 teaspoon salt

For the Bowl:

- Mixed greens (spinach, kale, arugula, etc.)
- Cherry tomatoes, halved
- Cucumber, sliced
- Avocado, sliced
- Red onion, thinly sliced
- Feta cheese, crumbled (optional)
- Lemon wedges for serving

For the Dressing:

- 2 tablespoons olive oil
- 1 tablespoon balsamic vinegar
- 1 teaspoon Dijon mustard
- Salt and pepper to taste

Instructions:

Prepare the Quinoa:

- Rinse the quinoa under cold water.
- In a medium saucepan, combine the quinoa, water or vegetable broth, and salt.
- Bring to a boil, then reduce the heat to low, cover, and simmer for 15-20 minutes or until the quinoa is cooked and the liquid is absorbed.
- Fluff the quinoa with a fork and set aside.

Prepare the Tuna:
- In a bowl, combine the drained tuna, olive oil, lemon juice, salt, and pepper. Mix well.

Prepare the Dressing:
- In a small bowl, whisk together the olive oil, balsamic vinegar, Dijon mustard, salt, and pepper.

Assemble the Bowl:
- In serving bowls, start with a base of cooked quinoa.
- Arrange mixed greens, cherry tomatoes, cucumber slices, avocado slices, and red onion on top of the quinoa.
- Spoon the tuna mixture over the veggies.

Drizzle with Dressing:
- Drizzle the prepared dressing over the entire bowl.

Optional Toppings:
- Add crumbled feta cheese on top for an extra burst of flavor.

Serve:
- Garnish with lemon wedges on the side and serve immediately.

Feel free to customize your tuna and quinoa bowl with additional vegetables, nuts, or seeds. This recipe offers a balance of protein, healthy fats, and wholesome grains, making it a satisfying and nutritious meal.

Tuna and Sundried Tomato Pesto Pasta

Ingredients:

- 8 ounces (about 225g) pasta (spaghetti, penne, or your choice)
- 1 can (about 5 ounces) tuna, drained
- 1/2 cup sun-dried tomatoes (packed in oil), chopped
- 2 tablespoons pine nuts
- 3 cloves garlic, minced
- 1/3 cup grated Parmesan cheese
- 1/2 cup fresh basil leaves, chopped
- 1/3 cup extra-virgin olive oil
- Salt and black pepper to taste
- Red pepper flakes (optional, for some heat)
- Freshly chopped parsley for garnish
- Grated Parmesan for serving

Instructions:

Cook the Pasta:
- Cook the pasta according to the package instructions in a large pot of salted boiling water until al dente. Drain and set aside.

Prepare the Sun-Dried Tomato Pesto:
- In a food processor, combine the sun-dried tomatoes, pine nuts, minced garlic, grated Parmesan, and fresh basil.
- While the food processor is running, gradually pour in the olive oil until the pesto reaches a smooth consistency.
- Season with salt and black pepper to taste. If you like some heat, you can add red pepper flakes.

Combine with Tuna:
- In a large mixing bowl, combine the drained tuna and cooked pasta.
- Add the sun-dried tomato pesto to the pasta and tuna, tossing until everything is well coated.

Adjust Seasoning:
- Taste and adjust the seasoning, adding more salt or pepper if needed.

Serve:
- Divide the tuna and sun-dried tomato pesto pasta among plates.

- Garnish with freshly chopped parsley and serve with extra grated Parmesan on the side.

This dish is not only delicious but also quick to prepare. The combination of tuna, sun-dried tomatoes, and pesto creates a savory and satisfying pasta experience. Feel free to customize the recipe by adding other ingredients like cherry tomatoes, olives, or spinach. Enjoy your flavorful tuna and sun-dried tomato pesto pasta!

Tuna and Potato Hash

Ingredients:

- 2 large potatoes, peeled and diced into small cubes
- 1 can (about 6-7 ounces) of tuna, drained
- 1 small onion, finely chopped
- 1 bell pepper, diced
- 2 cloves garlic, minced
- 2 tablespoons olive oil
- Salt and pepper to taste
- 1 teaspoon paprika (optional)
- Fresh parsley, chopped, for garnish (optional)
- Eggs (optional, for serving on top)

Instructions:

Boil Potatoes: Place the diced potatoes in a pot of salted water. Bring to a boil and cook until the potatoes are just tender, about 8-10 minutes. Drain and set aside.

Sauté Vegetables: In a large skillet, heat olive oil over medium heat. Add chopped onion, diced bell pepper, and minced garlic. Sauté until the vegetables are softened and fragrant.

Add Potatoes: Add the boiled diced potatoes to the skillet. Allow them to cook for a few minutes until they start to turn golden brown.

Incorporate Tuna: Gently fold in the drained tuna into the potato mixture. Stir well to combine.

Seasoning: Season the hash with salt, pepper, and paprika (if using). Adjust the seasoning to your taste.

Finish Cooking: Cook the hash for an additional 5-7 minutes, stirring occasionally, until everything is well combined and heated through.

Garnish: If desired, garnish the tuna and potato hash with fresh chopped parsley for a burst of freshness.

Optional Eggs: Serve the tuna and potato hash on its own or top it with a fried or poached egg for added richness and protein.

This Tuna and Potato Hash is versatile and can be customized based on your preferences. Feel free to add other vegetables, herbs, or spices to suit your taste. Enjoy your delicious and hearty meal!

Tuna and Cucumber Rolls

Ingredients:

- 1 can (about 6-7 ounces) of tuna, drained
- 1 cucumber
- 1/4 cup mayonnaise
- 1 tablespoon soy sauce
- 1 teaspoon rice vinegar
- 1 teaspoon sesame oil
- 1 teaspoon Sriracha sauce (optional, for a spicy kick)
- Salt and pepper to taste
- Nori sheets (seaweed sheets)
- Optional toppings: sesame seeds, avocado slices, chopped green onions

Instructions:

Prepare Tuna Filling:
- In a bowl, combine the drained tuna, mayonnaise, soy sauce, rice vinegar, sesame oil, Sriracha (if using), salt, and pepper. Mix well until the ingredients are thoroughly combined.

Prepare Cucumber:
- Peel the cucumber and cut it into thin, long strips using a vegetable peeler or a mandoline slicer. You want the strips to be thin enough to be pliable for rolling.

Assemble the Rolls:
- Place a sheet of nori on a clean surface or a bamboo sushi rolling mat.
- Lay cucumber strips on the nori, slightly overlapping, to create a solid layer.

Add Tuna Filling:
- Spoon the tuna mixture evenly along the length of the cucumber layer.

Rolling:
- Carefully roll the cucumber and tuna-filled nori sheet into a tight cylinder, similar to a sushi roll. Seal the edge with a bit of water.

Slice and Garnish:
- Using a sharp knife, slice the roll into bite-sized pieces. Arrange them on a plate.

- Optionally, garnish with sesame seeds, avocado slices, or chopped green onions.

Serve:
- Serve the tuna and cucumber rolls as they are or with a side of soy sauce for dipping.

These rolls are a great low-carb and gluten-free alternative to traditional sushi rolls. You can get creative with the fillings and customize them according to your preferences.

Enjoy your Tuna and Cucumber Rolls!

Tuna and Artichoke Dip

Ingredients:

- 1 can (about 6-7 ounces) of tuna, drained
- 1 can (about 14 ounces) of artichoke hearts, drained and chopped
- 1 cup mayonnaise
- 1 cup grated Parmesan cheese
- 1 cup shredded mozzarella cheese
- 1/2 cup sour cream
- 1/4 cup chopped green onions
- 1 clove garlic, minced
- 1 teaspoon lemon juice
- 1/2 teaspoon dried dill (optional)
- Salt and pepper to taste
- Tortilla chips, bread slices, or vegetable sticks for serving

Instructions:

Preheat Oven:
- Preheat your oven to 375°F (190°C).

Prepare Tuna and Artichoke Mixture:
- In a large mixing bowl, combine the drained tuna, chopped artichoke hearts, mayonnaise, grated Parmesan cheese, shredded mozzarella cheese, sour cream, chopped green onions, minced garlic, lemon juice, dried dill (if using), salt, and pepper. Mix well until all ingredients are evenly incorporated.

Transfer to Baking Dish:
- Grease a baking dish and transfer the tuna and artichoke mixture into it, spreading it out evenly.

Bake:
- Bake in the preheated oven for about 25-30 minutes or until the dip is hot and bubbly, and the top is golden brown.

Garnish and Serve:
- Once baked, remove the dip from the oven and garnish with additional chopped green onions or a sprinkle of Parmesan cheese if desired.

Serve Warm:
- Allow the dip to cool for a few minutes before serving. Serve it warm with tortilla chips, bread slices, or vegetable sticks.

This Tuna and Artichoke Dip is a crowd-pleaser and can be prepared in advance, making it convenient for entertaining guests. Feel free to adjust the ingredients to suit your taste preferences, and enjoy the creamy, flavorful dip!

Tuna and Egg Breakfast Burrito

Ingredients:

- 1 can (about 6-7 ounces) of tuna, drained
- 2 large eggs
- 1 tablespoon olive oil
- 1/4 cup diced onion
- 1/4 cup diced bell pepper (any color)
- 1/4 cup diced tomatoes
- 1/4 cup shredded cheese (cheddar, Monterey Jack, or your choice)
- Salt and pepper to taste
- 2 large flour tortillas
- Salsa or hot sauce (optional, for serving)
- Avocado slices (optional, for serving)
- Fresh cilantro, chopped (optional, for garnish)

Instructions:

Prepare Tuna:
- In a bowl, mix the drained tuna with a pinch of salt and pepper. Set aside.

Sauté Vegetables:
- In a skillet, heat olive oil over medium heat. Add diced onions and bell peppers. Sauté until the vegetables are softened.

Add Eggs:
- Push the sautéed vegetables to one side of the skillet. Crack the eggs into the empty side and scramble them. Once the eggs start to set, mix them with the sautéed vegetables.

Incorporate Tuna:
- Add the seasoned tuna to the egg and vegetable mixture. Stir well to combine. Cook for a few more minutes until the eggs are fully cooked and the tuna is heated through.

Assemble Burritos:
- Warm the tortillas in a dry skillet or microwave for a few seconds to make them pliable.
- Divide the tuna and egg mixture between the tortillas, placing it in the center.

Add Toppings:

- Sprinkle diced tomatoes and shredded cheese over the tuna and egg mixture.

Fold and Serve:
- Fold the sides of the tortilla over the filling and then roll it up into a burrito.

Garnish and Serve:
- Optionally, garnish with fresh cilantro. Serve the Tuna and Egg Breakfast Burritos with salsa, hot sauce, or avocado slices on the side.

This breakfast burrito is not only delicious but also customizable based on your preferences. Feel free to add other ingredients like sautéed mushrooms, spinach, or a dollop of sour cream. Enjoy your hearty breakfast!

Tuna and Rice Stuffed Tomatoes

Ingredients:

- 4 large tomatoes
- 1 cup cooked rice (white or brown)
- 1 can (about 6-7 ounces) of tuna, drained
- 1/4 cup red onion, finely chopped
- 1/4 cup cucumber, diced
- 1/4 cup bell pepper (any color), diced
- 2 tablespoons olive oil
- 2 tablespoons lemon juice
- 1 clove garlic, minced
- 2 tablespoons fresh parsley, chopped
- Salt and pepper to taste
- Grated Parmesan cheese (optional, for topping)
- Lemon wedges, for serving

Instructions:

Prepare Tomatoes:
- Cut the tops off the tomatoes and scoop out the seeds and pulp, leaving a tomato shell. You can use a spoon or a small knife for this.

Prepare Filling:
- In a bowl, combine the cooked rice, drained tuna, chopped red onion, diced cucumber, diced bell pepper, minced garlic, olive oil, lemon juice, chopped parsley, salt, and pepper. Mix well until all ingredients are evenly incorporated.

Stuff Tomatoes:
- Stuff each tomato with the tuna and rice mixture, pressing it down slightly.

Optional Cheese Topping:
- If desired, sprinkle a little grated Parmesan cheese on top of each stuffed tomato.

Bake:
- Place the stuffed tomatoes in a baking dish and bake in a preheated oven at 350°F (175°C) for about 15-20 minutes, or until the tomatoes are softened and the filling is heated through.

Garnish and Serve:

- Remove the stuffed tomatoes from the oven and garnish with additional chopped parsley. Serve them warm with lemon wedges on the side.

These tuna and rice stuffed tomatoes make a light and flavorful meal. You can experiment with the ingredients, adding herbs or additional vegetables according to your taste. Enjoy your delicious and wholesome stuffed tomatoes!

Tuna and Fennel Salad

Ingredients:

- 1 can (about 6-7 ounces) of tuna, drained
- 1 large fennel bulb, thinly sliced
- 1/2 red onion, thinly sliced
- 1 cup cherry tomatoes, halved
- 1/4 cup Kalamata olives, pitted and sliced
- 1/4 cup fresh parsley, chopped
- 2 tablespoons extra-virgin olive oil
- 1 tablespoon lemon juice
- 1 teaspoon Dijon mustard
- Salt and pepper to taste
- Optional: Feta cheese, crumbled, for garnish

Instructions:

Prepare Tuna:
- In a bowl, flake the drained tuna into bite-sized pieces.

Slice Fennel and Vegetables:
- Trim the fennel bulb, remove the tough outer layer, and thinly slice it. Thinly slice the red onion, halve the cherry tomatoes, and chop the fresh parsley.

Combine Ingredients:
- In a large salad bowl, combine the flaked tuna, sliced fennel, sliced red onion, halved cherry tomatoes, sliced Kalamata olives, and chopped parsley.

Prepare Dressing:
- In a small bowl, whisk together the extra-virgin olive oil, lemon juice, Dijon mustard, salt, and pepper to make the dressing.

Toss Salad:
- Pour the dressing over the tuna and fennel mixture. Toss everything together until well coated with the dressing.

Optional Cheese Garnish:
- If desired, sprinkle crumbled feta cheese on top of the salad for an extra burst of flavor.

Chill and Serve:

- Allow the salad to chill in the refrigerator for about 30 minutes to let the flavors meld. Serve chilled.

This Tuna and Fennel Salad is light, crisp, and perfect for a healthy lunch or dinner. Feel free to adjust the ingredients and quantities based on your preferences. Enjoy the refreshing combination of tuna and fennel!

Tuna and Corn Chowder

Ingredients:

- 2 cans (about 6-7 ounces each) of tuna, drained
- 1 onion, finely chopped
- 2 cloves garlic, minced
- 2 tablespoons butter or olive oil
- 1/4 cup all-purpose flour
- 4 cups chicken or vegetable broth
- 2 cups potatoes, peeled and diced
- 2 cups frozen or fresh corn kernels
- 1 cup carrots, diced
- 1 cup celery, diced
- 2 cups milk (whole or 2%)
- 1 cup heavy cream (optional, for a creamier chowder)
- Salt and pepper to taste
- 1 teaspoon dried thyme
- Fresh parsley, chopped, for garnish (optional)

Instructions:

Sauté Vegetables:
- In a large pot, melt the butter (or heat the olive oil) over medium heat. Add the chopped onion and garlic, sauté until softened.

Add Flour:
- Stir in the flour to create a roux. Cook for a couple of minutes to remove the raw taste of the flour.

Add Broth:
- Gradually whisk in the chicken or vegetable broth, ensuring there are no lumps.

Add Vegetables:
- Add the diced potatoes, corn kernels, diced carrots, and diced celery to the pot. Bring the mixture to a simmer.

Simmer:
- Simmer the chowder for about 15-20 minutes or until the vegetables are tender.

Add Tuna and Dairy:

- Stir in the drained tuna, milk, and heavy cream (if using). Season with salt, pepper, and dried thyme. Simmer for an additional 10 minutes to allow the flavors to meld.

Adjust Consistency and Seasoning:
- If the chowder is too thick, you can add more milk or broth to reach your desired consistency. Adjust the seasoning to taste.

Serve:
- Ladle the Tuna and Corn Chowder into bowls. Garnish with chopped fresh parsley if desired.

This Tuna and Corn Chowder is a comforting and satisfying meal. Feel free to customize it by adding other vegetables or herbs according to your taste preferences.

Enjoy your warm and flavorful chowder!

Tuna and Mango Salsa Tacos

Ingredients:

Tuna Filling:

- 2 cans (about 6-7 ounces each) of tuna, drained
- 2 tablespoons mayonnaise
- 1 tablespoon lime juice
- 1 teaspoon ground cumin
- Salt and pepper to taste

Mango Salsa:

- 1 ripe mango, peeled, pitted, and diced
- 1/2 red onion, finely chopped
- 1 jalapeño, seeded and finely chopped
- 1/4 cup fresh cilantro, chopped
- 1 tablespoon lime juice
- Salt to taste

Tacos:

- Small flour or corn tortillas
- Shredded lettuce or cabbage
- Avocado slices
- Sour cream (optional)
- Lime wedges for serving

Optional Garnish:

- Crumbled queso fresco or feta cheese
- Chopped fresh cilantro

Instructions:

Prepare Tuna Filling:
- In a bowl, combine the drained tuna, mayonnaise, lime juice, ground cumin, salt, and pepper. Mix well until the ingredients are thoroughly combined. Set aside.

Make Mango Salsa:
- In another bowl, combine the diced mango, chopped red onion, jalapeño, cilantro, lime juice, and salt. Toss to mix. Adjust salt and lime juice to taste.

Assemble Tacos:
- Warm the tortillas in a dry skillet or microwave for a few seconds until pliable.
- Spread a generous spoonful of the tuna filling onto each tortilla.

Add Mango Salsa and Toppings:
- Top the tuna with a spoonful of mango salsa.
- Add shredded lettuce or cabbage, avocado slices, and sour cream if desired.

Optional Garnish:
- Sprinkle crumbled queso fresco or feta cheese and chopped fresh cilantro on top for an extra burst of flavor.

Serve:
- Serve the Tuna and Mango Salsa Tacos with lime wedges on the side.

These tacos are not only delicious but also provide a perfect balance of flavors and textures. Feel free to adjust the ingredients and quantities based on your preferences. Enjoy the fusion of savory tuna and sweet mango salsa in every bite!

Tuna and Pesto Stuffed Peppers

Ingredients:

Tuna and Pesto Filling:

- 2 cans (about 6-7 ounces each) of tuna, drained
- 1/4 cup basil pesto
- 1/2 cup cherry tomatoes, diced
- 1/4 cup red onion, finely chopped
- 1/4 cup black olives, sliced
- Salt and pepper to taste

Peppers:

- 4 large bell peppers (any color)
- Olive oil for brushing

Optional Topping:

- Shredded mozzarella or Parmesan cheese

Garnish:

- Fresh basil leaves, chopped

Instructions:

Prepare Tuna and Pesto Filling:
- In a bowl, combine the drained tuna, basil pesto, diced cherry tomatoes, chopped red onion, sliced black olives, salt, and pepper. Mix well until all ingredients are evenly combined. Set aside.

Prepare Peppers:
- Preheat the oven to 375°F (190°C).
- Cut the bell peppers in half lengthwise, removing the seeds and membranes.
- Lightly brush the outside of the pepper halves with olive oil.

Stuff Peppers:
- Spoon the tuna and pesto filling into each pepper half, pressing it down slightly.

Optional Cheese Topping:

- If desired, sprinkle shredded mozzarella or Parmesan cheese on top of the stuffed peppers.

Bake:
- Place the stuffed peppers in a baking dish and bake in the preheated oven for about 20-25 minutes or until the peppers are tender and the filling is heated through.

Garnish:
- Remove the stuffed peppers from the oven and garnish with chopped fresh basil leaves.

Serve:
- Serve the Tuna and Pesto Stuffed Peppers warm. They can be enjoyed on their own or with a side salad for a complete meal.

This recipe provides a delicious combination of tuna, pesto, and Mediterranean-inspired flavors. Feel free to customize the filling or add additional ingredients based on your preferences. Enjoy your tasty and nutritious stuffed peppers!

Tuna and Lemon Risotto

Ingredients:

- 1 cup Arborio rice
- 1 can (about 6-7 ounces) of tuna, drained and flaked
- 1/2 cup dry white wine (optional)
- 4 cups chicken or vegetable broth, kept warm
- 1 small onion, finely chopped
- 2 cloves garlic, minced
- 1/2 cup Parmesan cheese, grated
- 2 tablespoons butter
- 2 tablespoons olive oil
- Zest of 1 lemon
- Juice of 1 lemon
- Salt and pepper to taste
- Fresh parsley, chopped, for garnish

Instructions:

Prepare Broth:
- Warm the chicken or vegetable broth in a separate pot and keep it at a simmer.

Sauté Onion and Garlic:
- In a large, deep skillet or saucepan, heat the olive oil over medium heat. Add the chopped onion and sauté until translucent. Add the minced garlic and cook for another 1-2 minutes.

Toast Rice:
- Add the Arborio rice to the skillet and stir to coat it with the oil. Toast the rice for 1-2 minutes until the edges become translucent.

Deglaze with Wine (Optional):
- Pour in the white wine and stir until it is mostly absorbed by the rice.

Add Broth:
- Begin adding the warm broth, one ladle at a time, stirring frequently. Wait until the liquid is mostly absorbed before adding the next ladle. Continue this process until the rice is creamy and cooked to al dente, which usually takes about 18-20 minutes.

Incorporate Tuna:

- When the risotto is almost done, gently fold in the drained and flaked tuna. Cook for an additional 2-3 minutes to heat the tuna.

Finish with Lemon:
- Stir in the lemon zest, lemon juice, Parmesan cheese, and butter. Season with salt and pepper to taste. Adjust the consistency with a little more broth if needed.

Garnish and Serve:
- Garnish the Tuna and Lemon Risotto with chopped fresh parsley. Serve immediately while it's hot.

This Tuna and Lemon Risotto is a bright and flavorful dish that can be enjoyed as a main course or as a side dish. Feel free to adjust the lemon and seasoning to suit your taste preferences. Enjoy your delicious homemade risotto!

Tuna and Watermelon Salad

Ingredients:

For the Salad:

- 2 cans (about 6-7 ounces each) of tuna, drained
- 4 cups seedless watermelon, cubed
- 1 cucumber, peeled and sliced
- 1/4 red onion, thinly sliced
- 1 cup feta cheese, crumbled
- Fresh mint leaves, chopped, for garnish
- Salt and black pepper to taste

For the Dressing:

- 3 tablespoons extra-virgin olive oil
- 2 tablespoons balsamic vinegar
- 1 tablespoon honey
- 1 teaspoon Dijon mustard
- Salt and black pepper to taste

Optional Additions:

- Kalamata olives, pitted and sliced
- Cherry tomatoes, halved
- Arugula or mixed salad greens

Instructions:

Prepare Tuna:
- In a bowl, flake the drained tuna into bite-sized pieces. Season with salt and black pepper to taste.

Prepare Watermelon and Vegetables:
- In a large salad bowl, combine the cubed watermelon, sliced cucumber, thinly sliced red onion, and crumbled feta cheese. If you're adding olives, tomatoes, or greens, include them at this stage.

Make Dressing:
- In a small bowl, whisk together the olive oil, balsamic vinegar, honey, Dijon mustard, salt, and black pepper to create the dressing.

Assemble Salad:
- Gently toss the flaked tuna into the watermelon and vegetable mixture.

Add Dressing:
- Drizzle the dressing over the salad and toss everything together until well coated.

Garnish:
- Garnish the Tuna and Watermelon Salad with fresh mint leaves.

Serve:
- Serve the salad immediately, allowing the flavors to meld. It's best enjoyed chilled.

This Tuna and Watermelon Salad is perfect for a light and summery meal. The sweetness of the watermelon pairs wonderfully with the savory tuna and the tangy dressing. Feel free to customize the salad with additional ingredients based on your preferences. Enjoy this unique and refreshing dish!

Tuna and Asparagus Quiche

Ingredients:

For the Quiche Filling:

- 1 can (about 6-7 ounces) of tuna, drained and flaked
- 1 cup fresh asparagus, trimmed and cut into bite-sized pieces
- 1/2 cup shredded Swiss or Gruyere cheese
- 1/4 cup grated Parmesan cheese
- 1/4 cup sun-dried tomatoes, chopped (optional)
- 1 tablespoon olive oil
- 1 small onion, finely chopped
- 3 cloves garlic, minced
- Salt and black pepper to taste

For the Quiche Custard:

- 4 large eggs
- 1 cup milk (whole or 2%)
- 1/2 cup heavy cream
- 1 teaspoon Dijon mustard
- Salt and black pepper to taste
- A pinch of nutmeg (optional)

For the Quiche Crust:

- 1 pre-made pie crust or homemade pie crust

Instructions:

Preheat Oven:
- Preheat your oven to 375°F (190°C).

Prepare Pie Crust:
- If using a pre-made pie crust, follow the package instructions for pre-baking. If using a homemade crust, roll it out and fit it into a pie dish, then pre-bake it for about 10 minutes until it's set but not fully cooked.

Sauté Asparagus and Onions:
- In a skillet, heat olive oil over medium heat. Add chopped onions and minced garlic, sauté until softened. Add asparagus pieces and cook for an additional 2-3 minutes until they are slightly tender. Remove from heat.

Prepare Quiche Filling:

- In a bowl, combine the flaked tuna, sautéed asparagus and onions, shredded Swiss or Gruyere cheese, grated Parmesan cheese, and sun-dried tomatoes (if using). Season with salt and black pepper. Mix well.

Prepare Quiche Custard:
- In another bowl, whisk together eggs, milk, heavy cream, Dijon mustard, salt, black pepper, and nutmeg (if using).

Assemble Quiche:
- Spread the tuna and asparagus filling evenly over the pre-baked pie crust. Pour the custard mixture over the filling.

Bake:
- Bake in the preheated oven for 35-40 minutes or until the quiche is set and golden brown on top.

Cool and Serve:
- Allow the quiche to cool for a few minutes before slicing. Serve warm.

This Tuna and Asparagus Quiche makes for a delicious brunch or lunch option. Feel free to customize the ingredients or add herbs like thyme or dill for additional flavor. Enjoy your savory and satisfying quiche!

Tuna and Mushroom Stroganoff

Ingredients:

- 2 cans (about 6-7 ounces each) of tuna, drained
- 8 oz (about 225g) mushrooms, sliced
- 1 onion, finely chopped
- 2 cloves garlic, minced
- 2 tablespoons olive oil
- 2 tablespoons all-purpose flour
- 1 cup beef or vegetable broth
- 1 tablespoon Worcestershire sauce
- 1 teaspoon Dijon mustard
- 1/2 cup sour cream
- Salt and pepper to taste
- Fresh parsley, chopped, for garnish
- Cooked egg noodles or rice, for serving

Instructions:

Prepare Tuna:
- Flake the drained tuna into bite-sized pieces and set aside.

Sauté Mushrooms and Onions:
- In a large skillet, heat olive oil over medium heat. Add chopped onions and sliced mushrooms. Sauté until the vegetables are softened and the mushrooms release their moisture.

Add Garlic:
- Add minced garlic to the skillet and sauté for an additional minute until fragrant.

Make Roux:
- Sprinkle flour over the mushroom mixture and stir to create a roux. Cook for 1-2 minutes to eliminate the raw flour taste.

Deglaze with Broth:
- Gradually add the broth to the skillet, stirring constantly to avoid lumps. Bring the mixture to a simmer.

Add Tuna and Flavors:

- Stir in the flaked tuna, Worcestershire sauce, Dijon mustard, salt, and pepper. Allow the mixture to simmer for about 5-7 minutes, allowing the flavors to meld.

Finish with Sour Cream:
- Reduce heat to low and stir in the sour cream. Cook for an additional 2-3 minutes, ensuring the sauce is heated through but not boiling.

Adjust Seasoning:
- Taste the stroganoff and adjust the seasoning if needed.

Serve:
- Serve the Tuna and Mushroom Stroganoff over cooked egg noodles or rice. Garnish with chopped fresh parsley.

This Tuna and Mushroom Stroganoff is a creamy, savory dish that can be served as a comforting weeknight dinner. Feel free to customize it with your favorite herbs and spices. Enjoy your delicious meal!

Tuna and Roasted Red Pepper Sandwich

Ingredients:

- 1 can (about 6-7 ounces) of tuna, drained
- 1/4 cup mayonnaise
- 2 tablespoons Greek yogurt or sour cream
- 1 tablespoon Dijon mustard
- Salt and pepper to taste
- 4 slices whole-grain bread or your favorite bread
- 1/2 cup roasted red peppers, sliced (store-bought or homemade)
- 1 cup arugula or baby spinach
- 4 slices provolone or Swiss cheese (optional)
- Olive oil (optional, for drizzling)
- Optional additions: sliced tomatoes, red onion, or avocado

Instructions:

Prepare Tuna Salad:
- In a bowl, combine the drained tuna, mayonnaise, Greek yogurt or sour cream, Dijon mustard, salt, and pepper. Mix well until all ingredients are thoroughly combined.

Assemble Sandwich:
- Toast the bread slices if desired. Spread the tuna salad evenly on each slice of bread.

Add Roasted Red Peppers:
- Layer the sliced roasted red peppers over the tuna salad on two of the bread slices.

Add Greens and Cheese:
- Top the roasted red peppers with a handful of arugula or baby spinach. If using cheese, place a slice on top of the greens.

Optional Additions:
- If desired, add sliced tomatoes, red onion, or avocado to the sandwich.

Assemble Sandwich:
- Place the other slices of bread on top to complete the sandwiches.

Drizzle with Olive Oil (Optional):
- For extra flavor, drizzle a bit of olive oil over the assembled sandwiches.

Serve:

- Cut the sandwiches in half diagonally and serve immediately.

This Tuna and Roasted Red Pepper Sandwich is a satisfying and flavorful option for lunch or a quick dinner. Feel free to customize it with your favorite ingredients and enjoy!

Tuna and Green Bean Almondine

Ingredients:

- 2 cans (about 6-7 ounces each) of tuna, drained and flaked
- 1 pound fresh green beans, ends trimmed
- 2 tablespoons olive oil
- 2 tablespoons butter
- 1/2 cup sliced almonds
- 2 cloves garlic, minced
- 1 tablespoon lemon juice
- Salt and pepper to taste
- Fresh parsley, chopped, for garnish (optional)
- Lemon wedges, for serving

Instructions:

Blanch Green Beans:
- Bring a large pot of salted water to a boil. Add the trimmed green beans and cook for 2-3 minutes until they are bright green and crisp-tender. Quickly transfer the green beans to a bowl of ice water to stop the cooking process. Drain and set aside.

Toast Almonds:
- In a large skillet, heat the olive oil over medium heat. Add the sliced almonds and toast them until they are golden brown, stirring frequently to avoid burning. Once toasted, transfer the almonds to a plate and set aside.

Sauté Garlic:
- In the same skillet, add the butter over medium heat. Add the minced garlic and sauté for about 1 minute until fragrant.

Add Green Beans:
- Add the blanched green beans to the skillet. Toss them in the garlic butter until they are well-coated and heated through.

Incorporate Tuna:
- Add the flaked tuna to the skillet. Gently toss the tuna with the green beans until evenly distributed and heated.

Season and Finish:
- Drizzle the lemon juice over the tuna and green bean mixture. Season with salt and pepper to taste. Toss everything together until well combined.

Serve:
- Transfer the Tuna and Green Bean Almondine to a serving platter. Sprinkle the toasted almonds over the top. Garnish with chopped fresh parsley if desired.

Serve with Lemon Wedges:
- Serve the dish with lemon wedges on the side for an extra burst of citrus flavor.

This Tuna and Green Bean Almondine makes for a light and flavorful meal. It's perfect for a quick and healthy lunch or dinner. Enjoy!

Tuna and Dill Cucumber Bites

Ingredients:

- 1 can (about 6-7 ounces) of tuna, drained
- 1/4 cup mayonnaise
- 1 tablespoon Greek yogurt or sour cream
- 1 tablespoon fresh dill, chopped
- 1 teaspoon Dijon mustard
- Salt and pepper to taste
- English cucumber, sliced into rounds
- Optional: Cherry tomatoes, sliced olives, or capers for garnish

Instructions:

Prepare Tuna Salad:
- In a bowl, combine the drained tuna, mayonnaise, Greek yogurt or sour cream, chopped fresh dill, Dijon mustard, salt, and pepper. Mix well until all ingredients are thoroughly combined.

Assemble Cucumber Bites:
- Slice the English cucumber into rounds, creating a base for your bites.

Top with Tuna Salad:
- Spoon a small amount of the tuna salad onto each cucumber round.

Garnish (Optional):
- If desired, garnish each bite with a slice of cherry tomato, sliced olives, or capers for added flavor and color.

Serve:
- Arrange the Tuna and Dill Cucumber Bites on a serving platter and serve immediately.

These bites are not only tasty but also low-carb and keto-friendly. They make for a perfect appetizer for parties or a light and refreshing snack. Feel free to adjust the quantities and ingredients based on your preferences. Enjoy your Tuna and Dill Cucumber Bites!

Tuna and Pineapple Skewers

Ingredients:

- 1 can (about 6-7 ounces) of tuna, drained
- 1 cup fresh pineapple chunks
- 1 red bell pepper, cut into chunks
- 1 green bell pepper, cut into chunks
- Wooden skewers, soaked in water for 30 minutes
- 2 tablespoons soy sauce
- 1 tablespoon honey or maple syrup
- 1 tablespoon olive oil
- 1 teaspoon fresh ginger, grated
- 1 clove garlic, minced
- Salt and pepper to taste
- Optional: Sesame seeds and chopped cilantro for garnish

Instructions:

Prepare Tuna Marinade:
- In a bowl, mix together soy sauce, honey (or maple syrup), olive oil, grated ginger, minced garlic, salt, and pepper. This will be your marinade.

Marinate Tuna:
- Place the drained tuna in the marinade, ensuring it is well-coated. Allow it to marinate for at least 15-30 minutes.

Preheat Grill or Oven:
- Preheat your grill or oven broiler.

Assemble Skewers:
- Thread the marinated tuna, pineapple chunks, and bell pepper pieces onto the soaked wooden skewers, alternating the ingredients.

Grill or Broil:
- Grill or broil the skewers for about 2-3 minutes on each side, or until the tuna is cooked to your liking and the pineapple and peppers are slightly caramelized.

Optional Garnish:
- If desired, garnish the Tuna and Pineapple Skewers with sesame seeds and chopped cilantro.

Serve:

- Arrange the skewers on a platter and serve them as a tasty appetizer or snack.

These Tuna and Pineapple Skewers offer a perfect blend of sweet and savory flavors with a hint of tropical goodness. They are quick to make and ideal for summer grilling or any time you want a flavorful and healthy bite. Enjoy!

Tuna and Sweet Potato Hash

Ingredients:

- 2 cans (about 6-7 ounces each) of tuna, drained
- 2 medium-sized sweet potatoes, peeled and diced into small cubes
- 1 red bell pepper, diced
- 1 yellow onion, diced
- 2 cloves garlic, minced
- 2 tablespoons olive oil
- 1 teaspoon paprika
- 1/2 teaspoon cumin
- Salt and pepper to taste
- Fresh parsley, chopped, for garnish (optional)
- Eggs (optional, for serving on top)

Instructions:

Prepare Sweet Potatoes:
- Peel and dice the sweet potatoes into small cubes.

Sauté Vegetables:
- In a large skillet, heat olive oil over medium heat. Add diced sweet potatoes, diced bell pepper, and diced onion. Sauté until the vegetables are softened and slightly caramelized, about 10-12 minutes.

Add Garlic and Spices:
- Add minced garlic, paprika, cumin, salt, and pepper to the skillet. Stir and cook for an additional 1-2 minutes until the garlic is fragrant and the spices are well incorporated.

Incorporate Tuna:
- Add the drained tuna to the skillet. Gently fold it into the sweet potato mixture and cook for another 2-3 minutes until the tuna is heated through.

Optional: Cook Eggs (for serving on top):
- If you like, you can cook eggs separately (fried, poached, or scrambled) and serve them on top of the hash.

Garnish and Serve:
- Garnish the Tuna and Sweet Potato Hash with chopped fresh parsley if desired. Serve warm.

This Tuna and Sweet Potato Hash is a flavorful and filling dish. It's versatile, and you can customize it by adding your favorite herbs or spices. Enjoy this hearty and nutritious meal!

Tuna and Roasted Garlic Hummus Wrap

Ingredients:

- 1 can (about 6-7 ounces) of tuna, drained
- 1/2 cup roasted garlic hummus
- 4 whole wheat or spinach tortillas
- 1 cup mixed salad greens (e.g., arugula, spinach, or lettuce)
- 1 cucumber, thinly sliced
- 1 tomato, sliced
- Red onion, thinly sliced (optional)
- Kalamata olives, sliced (optional)
- Feta cheese, crumbled (optional)
- Salt and pepper to taste

Instructions:

Prepare Tuna:
- In a bowl, flake the drained tuna into bite-sized pieces. Season with salt and pepper to taste.

Assemble Wraps:
- Lay out the tortillas on a clean surface.
- Spread a generous layer of roasted garlic hummus over each tortilla.

Add Tuna and Vegetables:
- Divide the flaked tuna evenly among the tortillas, placing it in the center of each one.
- Top the tuna with mixed salad greens, cucumber slices, tomato slices, and any other optional toppings you desire, such as red onion, Kalamata olives, or crumbled feta cheese.

Fold and Serve:
- Fold the sides of the tortilla over the filling and then roll it up into a wrap.

Optional: Grill or Warm Wraps (Optional):
- If you prefer, you can warm the wraps in a skillet or grill pan for a few minutes on each side until lightly toasted.

Serve:
- Cut the wraps in half diagonally and serve immediately.

These Tuna and Roasted Garlic Hummus Wraps are not only delicious but also packed with protein and veggies. Feel free to customize the wraps with your favorite ingredients and enjoy a flavorful and nutritious meal!

Tuna and Cilantro Lime Rice Bowl

Ingredients:

For the Tuna:

- 2 cans (about 6-7 ounces each) of tuna, drained
- 2 tablespoons soy sauce
- 1 tablespoon sesame oil
- 1 tablespoon rice vinegar
- 1 teaspoon honey or maple syrup
- 1 teaspoon grated ginger
- 1 clove garlic, minced
- Sesame seeds for garnish (optional)

For the Cilantro Lime Rice:

- 2 cups cooked rice (white or brown)
- 1/4 cup fresh cilantro, chopped
- 1 lime, juiced
- Salt to taste

Bowl Toppings:

- Sliced avocado
- Shredded carrots
- Sliced cucumber
- Red cabbage, thinly sliced
- Green onions, chopped
- Sriracha or your favorite hot sauce (optional)

Instructions:

Prepare Tuna:
- In a bowl, whisk together soy sauce, sesame oil, rice vinegar, honey or maple syrup, grated ginger, and minced garlic.
- Add the drained tuna to the marinade, tossing gently to coat. Allow it to marinate while you prepare the rice and toppings.

Make Cilantro Lime Rice:

- In another bowl, combine the cooked rice with chopped cilantro, lime juice, and salt. Mix well.

Assemble the Bowl:
- Divide the cilantro lime rice among serving bowls.
- Top the rice with marinated tuna.

Add Toppings:
- Arrange sliced avocado, shredded carrots, sliced cucumber, thinly sliced red cabbage, and chopped green onions on top of the tuna.

Garnish:
- Garnish with sesame seeds if desired.

Optional: Drizzle with Sriracha:
- If you like some heat, drizzle Sriracha or your favorite hot sauce over the bowl.

Serve:
- Serve the Tuna and Cilantro Lime Rice Bowl immediately, allowing each person to mix the ingredients together before enjoying.

This Tuna and Cilantro Lime Rice Bowl is not only delicious but also customizable based on your preferences. Feel free to add or substitute ingredients to suit your taste. Enjoy your flavorful and nutritious meal!

Tuna and Blue Cheese Flatbread

Ingredients:

For the Tuna:

- 2 cans (about 6-7 ounces each) of tuna, drained
- 2 tablespoons mayonnaise
- 1 tablespoon Dijon mustard
- 1 tablespoon lemon juice
- Salt and pepper to taste

For the Blue Cheese Sauce:

- 1/2 cup blue cheese, crumbled
- 1/4 cup sour cream
- 1 tablespoon mayonnaise
- 1 teaspoon lemon juice
- Salt and pepper to taste

For the Flatbread:

- Store-bought flatbread or naan
- Olive oil for brushing
- Garlic powder (optional, for extra flavor)
- Fresh arugula or baby spinach for topping
- Cherry tomatoes, halved
- Red onion, thinly sliced
- Balsamic glaze for drizzling

Instructions:

Prepare Tuna:
- In a bowl, mix together the drained tuna, mayonnaise, Dijon mustard, lemon juice, salt, and pepper. Set aside.

Make Blue Cheese Sauce:
- In another bowl, combine crumbled blue cheese, sour cream, mayonnaise, lemon juice, salt, and pepper. Mix until well combined.

Preheat Oven:
- Preheat your oven to the temperature specified on the flatbread or naan package.

Prepare Flatbread:
- Place the flatbread or naan on a baking sheet. Brush the surface with olive oil and sprinkle with garlic powder if desired.

Assemble Flatbread:
- Spread the tuna mixture evenly over the flatbread.

Add Blue Cheese Sauce:
- Spoon dollops of the blue cheese sauce over the tuna.

Bake:
- Bake the flatbread in the preheated oven according to the package instructions or until the edges are golden and the toppings are heated through.

Top with Fresh Greens and Vegetables:
- Remove the flatbread from the oven and top it with fresh arugula or baby spinach, halved cherry tomatoes, and thinly sliced red onion.

Drizzle with Balsamic Glaze:
- Finish by drizzling balsamic glaze over the top.

Slice and Serve:
- Slice the Tuna and Blue Cheese Flatbread into pieces and serve immediately.

This Tuna and Blue Cheese Flatbread offers a delightful combination of textures and flavors. It makes for a unique and satisfying meal that can be enjoyed as a light lunch or dinner. Feel free to customize the toppings to suit your preferences. Enjoy!

Tuna and Mango Avocado Rolls

Ingredients:

For the Tuna Filling:

- 2 cans (about 6-7 ounces each) of tuna, drained
- 2 tablespoons mayonnaise
- 1 tablespoon soy sauce
- 1 teaspoon sriracha sauce (adjust to taste)
- 1 teaspoon sesame oil
- 1 green onion, finely chopped

For the Rolls:

- Nori (seaweed) sheets
- Sushi rice (prepared according to package instructions, seasoned with rice vinegar, sugar, and salt)
- 1 ripe mango, peeled, pitted, and sliced into thin strips
- 1 ripe avocado, peeled, pitted, and sliced
- Cucumber, julienned
- Pickled ginger, for serving
- Soy sauce, for dipping

Optional for Garnish:

- Sesame seeds
- Chopped cilantro

Instructions:

Prepare Tuna Filling:
- In a bowl, combine the drained tuna, mayonnaise, soy sauce, sriracha sauce, sesame oil, and chopped green onion. Mix well and set aside.

Prepare Sushi Rice:
- Cook sushi rice according to the package instructions. Once cooked, season the rice with a mixture of rice vinegar, sugar, and salt. Let it cool.

Assemble Rolls:

- Place a bamboo sushi rolling mat on a flat surface and put a sheet of plastic wrap on top. Lay a nori sheet, shiny side down, onto the plastic wrap.
- Wet your hands to prevent sticking, and spread a thin layer of sushi rice over the nori, leaving a small border at the top.
- Place tuna filling, mango strips, avocado slices, and julienned cucumber in the center of the rice.

Roll Up:
- Carefully lift the edge of the bamboo mat closest to you, and begin rolling the nori and rice over the filling. Apply gentle pressure to shape the roll.
- Continue rolling until you reach the uncovered border. Wet the border with a bit of water and seal the edge.

Slice Rolls:
- Using a sharp knife dipped in water, slice the rolled sushi into bite-sized pieces.

Garnish and Serve:
- Garnish the Tuna and Mango Avocado Rolls with sesame seeds and chopped cilantro if desired.

Serve with Dipping Sauce:
- Serve the rolls with soy sauce and pickled ginger on the side for dipping.

These Tuna and Mango Avocado Rolls offer a delightful combination of flavors and textures. They make for a light and healthy meal, perfect for a sushi night at home. Enjoy your homemade sushi rolls!

Tuna and Cornbread Casserole

Ingredients:

For the Cornbread:

- 1 cup yellow cornmeal
- 1 cup all-purpose flour
- 1 tablespoon baking powder
- 1/2 teaspoon baking soda
- 1/2 teaspoon salt
- 1 cup buttermilk
- 1/4 cup unsalted butter, melted
- 1/4 cup honey
- 2 large eggs

For the Tuna Filling:

- 2 cans (about 6-7 ounces each) of tuna, drained
- 1/2 cup mayonnaise
- 1 tablespoon Dijon mustard
- 1/2 cup celery, finely chopped
- 1/4 cup red onion, finely chopped
- 1/4 cup dill pickles, finely chopped
- Salt and pepper to taste
- 1 cup shredded cheddar cheese (for topping)

Instructions:

Preheat Oven:
- Preheat your oven to 375°F (190°C). Grease a baking dish (9x13 inches or similar size).

Prepare Cornbread Batter:
- In a large bowl, whisk together cornmeal, flour, baking powder, baking soda, and salt.
- In another bowl, whisk together buttermilk, melted butter, honey, and eggs.
- Pour the wet ingredients into the dry ingredients and stir until just combined. Do not overmix.

Make Tuna Filling:

- In a separate bowl, mix together drained tuna, mayonnaise, Dijon mustard, chopped celery, chopped red onion, chopped dill pickles, salt, and pepper.

Assemble Casserole:
- Pour half of the cornbread batter into the prepared baking dish.
- Spread the tuna filling evenly over the cornbread layer.
- Top with the remaining cornbread batter, spreading it to cover the tuna filling.

Bake:
- Bake in the preheated oven for 25-30 minutes or until the cornbread is golden brown and a toothpick inserted into the center comes out clean.

Top with Cheese:
- Sprinkle shredded cheddar cheese over the top during the last 5 minutes of baking until melted and bubbly.

Cool and Serve:
- Allow the casserole to cool for a few minutes before slicing. Serve warm.

This Tuna and Cornbread Casserole is a comforting and wholesome dish that combines the goodness of cornbread with a tasty tuna filling. It's a perfect option for a family dinner or potluck. Enjoy!

Tuna and Cranberry Quinoa Salad

Ingredients:

For the Salad:

- 1 cup quinoa, rinsed
- 2 cans (about 6-7 ounces each) of tuna, drained and flaked
- 1/2 cup dried cranberries
- 1/4 cup red onion, finely chopped
- 1/4 cup fresh parsley, chopped
- 1/4 cup feta cheese, crumbled (optional)
- Salt and pepper to taste

For the Dressing:

- 3 tablespoons olive oil
- 2 tablespoons balsamic vinegar
- 1 tablespoon Dijon mustard
- 1 tablespoon honey or maple syrup
- Salt and pepper to taste

Optional Additions:

- 1 cucumber, diced
- Cherry tomatoes, halved
- Avocado, diced
- Almonds or walnuts, chopped

Instructions:

Cook Quinoa:
- In a medium saucepan, combine quinoa with 2 cups of water. Bring to a boil, then reduce the heat to low, cover, and simmer for 15-20 minutes or until the quinoa is cooked and the water is absorbed. Fluff with a fork and let it cool.

Prepare Dressing:
- In a small bowl, whisk together olive oil, balsamic vinegar, Dijon mustard, honey or maple syrup, salt, and pepper to create the dressing.

Assemble Salad:

- In a large salad bowl, combine the cooked quinoa, flaked tuna, dried cranberries, chopped red onion, fresh parsley, and crumbled feta cheese (if using).

Optional Additions:
- Add diced cucumber, halved cherry tomatoes, diced avocado, or chopped nuts if desired.

Drizzle with Dressing:
- Pour the dressing over the salad and toss gently until all ingredients are well coated.

Season:
- Season with salt and pepper to taste.

Chill and Serve:
- Refrigerate the Tuna and Cranberry Quinoa Salad for at least 30 minutes to allow the flavors to meld. Serve chilled.

This Tuna and Cranberry Quinoa Salad is not only delicious but also versatile. Feel free to customize it with your favorite vegetables and nuts. It makes for a wholesome and satisfying meal, perfect for lunch or a light dinner. Enjoy!

Tuna and Tomato Bruschetta

Ingredients:

- 1 can (about 6-7 ounces) of tuna, drained and flaked
- 2 large tomatoes, diced
- 1/4 cup red onion, finely chopped
- 2 cloves garlic, minced
- 1/4 cup fresh basil, chopped
- 2 tablespoons extra-virgin olive oil
- 1 tablespoon balsamic vinegar
- Salt and pepper to taste
- Baguette or Italian bread, sliced
- Olive oil for brushing the bread
- Optional: Balsamic glaze for drizzling

Instructions:

Prepare Tuna:
- In a bowl, combine the drained and flaked tuna with diced tomatoes, chopped red onion, minced garlic, and fresh basil.

Make Dressing:
- In a small bowl, whisk together extra-virgin olive oil, balsamic vinegar, salt, and pepper.

Combine Tuna and Dressing:
- Pour the dressing over the tuna and tomato mixture. Gently toss to combine, ensuring the ingredients are well coated.

Prepare Bread:
- Preheat your oven broiler. Brush the sliced baguette or Italian bread with olive oil on both sides.

Broil Bread:
- Place the bread slices on a baking sheet and broil for 1-2 minutes on each side, or until they are golden and slightly crisp.

Assemble Bruschetta:
- Spoon the tuna and tomato mixture onto the toasted bread slices.

Optional Drizzle:
- Drizzle with balsamic glaze if desired for extra flavor.

Serve:

- Arrange the Tuna and Tomato Bruschetta on a serving platter and serve immediately.

This Tuna and Tomato Bruschetta is a flavorful and elegant appetizer that can be served at parties or enjoyed as a light meal. The combination of tuna, tomatoes, and fresh herbs creates a burst of delicious flavors. Enjoy your bruschetta!

Tuna and Basil Pesto Panini

Ingredients:

For the Basil Pesto:

- 2 cups fresh basil leaves, packed
- 1/2 cup freshly grated Parmesan cheese
- 1/2 cup pine nuts or walnuts
- 3 garlic cloves, peeled
- 1/2 cup extra-virgin olive oil
- Salt and pepper to taste

For the Panini:

- 2 cans (about 6-7 ounces each) of tuna, drained
- 1/2 cup cherry tomatoes, sliced
- 4 slices of your favorite bread (ciabatta, baguette, or panini bread work well)
- 4 slices of mozzarella or provolone cheese
- Butter or olive oil for grilling

Instructions:

Prepare Basil Pesto:

> In a food processor, combine basil, Parmesan cheese, pine nuts or walnuts, and garlic cloves.
> Pulse until finely chopped.
> With the processor running, slowly pour in the olive oil until the mixture forms a smooth paste.
> Season with salt and pepper to taste. Set aside.

Assemble the Panini:

> Preheat your panini press or grill pan.
> In a bowl, mix the drained tuna with a few tablespoons of the prepared basil pesto. Adjust the amount to your taste.
> Lay out the slices of bread. Spread a generous amount of basil pesto on one side of each slice.
> Place a slice of mozzarella or provolone on two of the slices.
> Spoon the tuna mixture onto the cheese-covered slices.

Add sliced cherry tomatoes on top of the tuna.
Top with the remaining slices of bread, pesto side down, creating sandwiches.
Lightly butter or brush the outside of each sandwich with olive oil.
Grill the panini in the press or on a grill pan until the bread is toasted, and the cheese is melted (usually 3-5 minutes).
Carefully remove from the press or pan, slice, and serve hot.

Feel free to customize this recipe by adding additional ingredients like roasted red peppers, spinach, or artichoke hearts. Enjoy your delicious Tuna and Basil Pesto Panini!

Tuna and Roasted Vegetable Salad

Ingredients:

For the Salad:

- 2 cans (about 6-7 ounces each) of tuna, drained and flaked
- 4 cups mixed salad greens (e.g., spinach, arugula, or mixed baby greens)
- 1 cup cherry tomatoes, halved
- 1 cucumber, sliced
- 1 red bell pepper, sliced
- 1 yellow bell pepper, sliced
- 1 red onion, thinly sliced
- 1 zucchini, sliced
- 1 tablespoon olive oil
- Salt and pepper to taste

For the Dressing:

- 3 tablespoons olive oil
- 2 tablespoons balsamic vinegar
- 1 teaspoon Dijon mustard
- 1 clove garlic, minced
- Salt and pepper to taste

Optional Toppings:

- Feta cheese, crumbled
- Kalamata olives, pitted and sliced
- Fresh basil or parsley, chopped

Instructions:

Roast the Vegetables:

> Preheat the oven to 400°F (200°C).
> In a large bowl, toss the sliced red and yellow bell peppers, red onion, and zucchini with olive oil, salt, and pepper.
> Spread the vegetables on a baking sheet in a single layer.
> Roast in the preheated oven for about 20-25 minutes or until the vegetables are tender and slightly caramelized. Stir halfway through the roasting time.
> Remove from the oven and let the vegetables cool slightly.

Prepare the Dressing:

> In a small bowl, whisk together olive oil, balsamic vinegar, Dijon mustard, minced garlic, salt, and pepper. Set aside.

Assemble the Salad:

> In a large salad bowl, combine the mixed salad greens, cherry tomatoes, and cucumber.
> Add the roasted vegetables and flaked tuna to the salad.
> Drizzle the dressing over the salad and toss gently to combine.
> Optional: Top the salad with crumbled feta cheese, sliced Kalamata olives, and chopped fresh basil or parsley.
> Serve the Tuna and Roasted Vegetable Salad immediately, or refrigerate until ready to serve.

This salad is not only nutritious but also versatile. Feel free to customize it by adding your favorite vegetables or toppings. Enjoy your Tuna and Roasted Vegetable Salad!

Tuna and Bacon Stuffed Mushrooms

Ingredients:

- 1 can (about 6-7 ounces) of tuna, drained
- 8 ounces cremini or button mushrooms, cleaned and stems removed
- 4 slices bacon, cooked and crumbled
- 1/4 cup mayonnaise
- 1/4 cup breadcrumbs
- 2 tablespoons grated Parmesan cheese
- 1 green onion, finely chopped
- 1 tablespoon fresh parsley, chopped
- Salt and pepper to taste
- Olive oil for drizzling

Instructions:

Preheat the oven to 375°F (190°C).

Clean the mushrooms and remove the stems. Place the mushroom caps on a baking sheet.

In a bowl, combine the drained tuna, crumbled bacon, mayonnaise, breadcrumbs, Parmesan cheese, green onion, and chopped parsley. Mix well.

Season the mixture with salt and pepper to taste.

Spoon the tuna and bacon mixture into the mushroom caps, pressing down gently.

Drizzle a bit of olive oil over the stuffed mushrooms.

Bake in the preheated oven for 15-20 minutes or until the mushrooms are tender and the filling is golden brown.

Remove from the oven and let them cool slightly before serving.

Optionally, garnish with additional chopped parsley or grated Parmesan cheese before serving.

Enjoy these Tuna and Bacon Stuffed Mushrooms as a tasty appetizer for a gathering or as a flavorful snack!

Tuna and Black Bean Burrito Bowl

Ingredients:

For the Tuna and Black Bean Mix:

- 2 cans (about 6-7 ounces each) of tuna, drained
- 1 can (15 ounces) black beans, drained and rinsed
- 1 tablespoon olive oil
- 1 teaspoon ground cumin
- 1 teaspoon chili powder
- Salt and pepper to taste
- Lime juice (optional)

For the Burrito Bowl:

- Cooked brown rice or quinoa
- Shredded lettuce or spinach
- Cherry tomatoes, halved
- Corn kernels (fresh or thawed if frozen)
- Avocado, sliced
- Red onion, finely chopped
- Fresh cilantro, chopped
- Greek yogurt or sour cream for topping

Instructions:

Prepare the Tuna and Black Bean Mix:

> In a skillet, heat olive oil over medium heat.
> Add drained tuna to the skillet, breaking it into smaller chunks with a spatula.
> Add black beans, ground cumin, chili powder, salt, and pepper. Stir well to combine.
> Cook for 5-7 minutes or until the mixture is heated through and flavors are well combined.
> Optional: Squeeze fresh lime juice over the mixture for added brightness. Set aside.

Assemble the Burrito Bowl:

> In serving bowls, layer cooked brown rice or quinoa as the base.
> Top with the Tuna and Black Bean mixture.
> Arrange shredded lettuce or spinach, halved cherry tomatoes, corn kernels, sliced avocado, and chopped red onion on top.

Garnish with fresh cilantro.
Add a dollop of Greek yogurt or sour cream on the side.
Optionally, squeeze more lime juice over the bowl before serving.
Mix everything together before eating or enjoy each component separately.

This Tuna and Black Bean Burrito Bowl is customizable, so feel free to add your favorite toppings or adjust the quantities based on your preferences. It's a wholesome and satisfying meal that's rich in protein and packed with flavors. Enjoy!

Tuna and Orange Glazed Salmon Skewers

Ingredients:

For the Tuna Skewers:

- 2 cans (about 6-7 ounces each) of tuna, drained and cut into chunks
- Wooden skewers, soaked in water for 30 minutes

For the Orange Glaze:

- 1/2 cup orange juice (freshly squeezed is best)
- 2 tablespoons soy sauce
- 2 tablespoons honey
- 1 tablespoon rice vinegar
- 1 teaspoon grated fresh ginger
- 1 clove garlic, minced
- Red pepper flakes (optional, for heat)
- Salt and pepper to taste

Instructions:

Prepare the Orange Glaze:
- In a small saucepan, combine orange juice, soy sauce, honey, rice vinegar, grated ginger, minced garlic, and red pepper flakes (if using). Bring the mixture to a simmer over medium heat.

Simmer and Reduce:
- Allow the glaze to simmer for 10-15 minutes or until it thickens and becomes syrupy. Stir occasionally. Season with salt and pepper to taste. Set aside to cool.

Prepare Tuna Skewers:
- Thread chunks of tuna onto the soaked wooden skewers.

Grill or Broil:
- Preheat the grill or broiler. Cook the tuna skewers for 2-3 minutes on each side or until they reach your desired level of doneness.

Glaze the Skewers:
- Brush the orange glaze onto the tuna skewers during the last minute of cooking on each side. Continue to brush the glaze on until the skewers are fully coated.

Serve:
- Remove the tuna skewers from the grill or broiler. Serve them warm, drizzled with any remaining orange glaze.

These Tuna Skewers with Orange Glaze offer a delightful combination of sweet, savory, and citrusy flavors. Enjoy this unique and tasty dish!

www.ingramcontent.com/pod-product-compliance
Lightning Source LLC
LaVergne TN
LVHW081608060526
838201LV00054B/2136